AN INTRODUCTION TO THE CATHOLIC CHARISMATIC RENEWAL

+ UPDATED AND EXPANDED +

JOHN AND THERESE BOUCHER

servant
AN IMPRINT OF
FRANCISCAN MEDIA
Cincinnati, Ohio

Imprimatur: Most Reverend Robert J. McManus, S.T.D.
Bishop of Worcester
December 28, 2016

Cover and book design by Mark Sullivan

ISBN (print): 978-1-63253-156-8
ISBN (ebook): 978-1-63253-157-5

Published by Servant, an imprint of
Franciscan Media
28 W. Liberty St.
Cincinnati, OH 45202
FranciscanMedia.org

Printed in the United States of America.
Printed on acid-free paper.
17 18 19 20 21   5 4 3 2 1

Come Holy Spirit, Living Flame of love.
You tenderly know my soul in its deepest part.
We are here face to face.
Perfect me by your will.
Break this web of obstacles between myself and you.
Burn, oh delectable flame, fingers of delicate touch;
Blazing, you change death to life, God's forgiveness,
Jesus Christ.
—St. John of the Cross, adapted by John Boucher

CONTENTS

Praying to the Holy Spirit seemed like a strange thing to do, almost like trying to capture fresh air in a bottle. "How is this even possible?" I wondered as I strolled along the wooded path behind the last building on campus. Then a light breeze meandered through my soul, leaving behind a haunting melody. "Maybe these few notes are a clue!" I thought.

I shared the tune with John, who combined it with a prayer to the Holy Spirit adapted from St. John of the Cross's poem "Living Flame": "Come, Holy Spirit, living flame of love...." We later posted the song on YouTube, where more than 150,000 have heard it. You can hear it there too.[1]

John had encountered the Spirit a few years earlier as a stressed-out college student on retreat. A friend sent him to pray in the chapel, and there the words of Psalm 23:1 took on the timbre of God's voice: "The Lord is my shepherd. I shall not want." John realized, on some new and primal level, that God loved him. God would fill the void of his deepest longings. The Spirit would reach down inside him, transforming and reshaping his life.

Have you encountered the Holy Spirit? Maybe you have been invited to a charismatic prayer meeting, the New Life in the Spirit Seminar, a healing Mass, a parish mission, a worship service, or Alpha in the Catholic Context. Maybe someone has shared a religious experience or a spontaneous prayer with you, and you are intrigued. Or perhaps you were baptized in the Spirit long ago and would like to reenter that relationship with the Father, Son, and Holy Spirit. Then this little book is for you. We welcome you as a reader and a fellow pilgrim on a spiritual journey.

Part One of this book invites you to take a look at the work of the Holy Spirit, including the charisms he gives to help us live for God and serve the Church. Part Two takes a fiftieth-anniversary look at the Catholic Charismatic Renewal, a movement of the Holy Spirit that has brought us and millions of others into a deeper life with God. There we review some events that mark the movement's foundation and growth. Part Three invites us to live as everyday charismatics, missionary disciples willing to receive and share the Good News of Jesus through God's Holy Spirit. And Part Four offers encouragement and direction for moving forward in the life of the Holy Spirit.

At the end of this book, you'll find a Resource Section to guide you to more information and events that will help you grow in the life of the Spirit. There is also a glossary of terms that are specific to discussions about charismatic life.

Throughout this booklet, we will offer encouraging testimonies from many who have surrendered to the Spirit. These inspiring stories from our brothers and sisters in Christ offer evidence of the work of the Holy Spirit today. He is ever changing us, molding us into the image of God. And so we pray:

Come, Holy Spirit.

Fill our hearts anew with Jesus.

Fan into flame the fire of your love within us.

We choose to welcome Jesus
at the center of our beings and at the heart of the Church.
And we choose the journey toward God, our Father,
through your strength. Amen.

Over the last fifty years and into the present, the Catholic Charismatic Renewal movement has touched people from all over the world and from many occupations, cultures, and backgrounds.

• Sharon woke up one morning half-deaf and unable to stand. Months later, she was diagnosed with Meniere's disease, which could mean permanent hearing loss. She writes:

"Although I was a serious Catholic at the time, I was also an emotional wreck and horrified of facing life without sound. Then a priest friend offered to pray with me for physical and spiritual healing. When I balked, he asked, 'Is Jesus Christ the same yesterday, today, and forever?' I answered yes, and he proceeded with the sacramental anointing.

"My terrified spirit was filled with profound peace. And now I was intrigued. More informal, charismatic prayer for healing happened the next day, and I was gifted with the baptism of the Holy Spirit. Hours later, my hearing returned."

• Ronald was first baptized in the Spirit at a Presbyterian youth conference, but he soon rejected God because of a lack of support, ugly pastoral scandals, and professors who questioned God's existence. He married a Catholic involved in the renewal, but faith still eluded him. Then came September 11, 2001, when he watched out his office window as smoke billowed from the Pentagon. He cried out to Jesus in prayer. He experienced a deep desire for Jesus's presence and the new life the Savior offers.

Shortly after that tragic day, Ronald decided to join the Catholic Church and also a charismatic prayer group. "Now," he writes, "I have a solid formation and have become a fervent evangelist, teacher, servant, and leader."

• Harriet was a choir member and loved to sing, especially while driving. But one day she could not remember the words of a favorite hymn, so she just sang freely to God until the Spirit touched her and gave her the gift of singing in tongues. Later she developed an enduring desire to read the Bible. God's Word is now Harriet's constant companion.

The list goes on: Connie received the power to forgive her abusive husband. Juan experienced an instantaneous healing of torn muscles in his shoulder. Joel went from being hooked on drugs to serving in a homeless shelter. Sr. Nancy feels led to pray for the specific needs of others and sees some unbelievable results.

International Catholic Charismatic Renewal Services (ICCRS) in Rome estimates that one hundred twenty million Roman Catholics have experienced charismatic renewal since 1967. Almost twenty million Catholics worldwide attend a charismatic prayer meeting or event each month. Wherever the Catholic Church is, there are charismatic Catholics. They participate in prayer groups, Bible studies, faith-sharing groups, conferences, healing Masses, covenant communities, evangelizing ministries, and social action groups. ICCRS notes that this diverse renewal of the Catholic Church is taking place in more than 238 countries.[2]

At the Heart of It All

Though people's experiences with charismatic renewal may differ, there are four central realities:

1. Ongoing personal conversion to Jesus Christ as Lord, through the presence and power of the Holy Spirit in everyday life.

2. Seeking, receiving, and fostering charisms (gifts) of the Holy Spirit, for service to the Church and the world.

3. Striving to grow in holiness through prayer, Scripture, the sacraments, study, and serving others.

4. Working for the evangelization and transformation of nominal Christians, of the unchurched, of cultures, and of societies.

Charismatic renewal flows from personal and communal experiences of the presence and the power of the Holy Spirit. These experiences often begin with the "release of the Spirit" or "renewal of the Spirit," although they are also rooted in earlier reception of the sacraments.

The *Catechism of the Catholic Church* tells us, "Sacraments are 'powers that come forth' from the Body of Christ, which is ever-living and life-giving. They are actions of the Holy Spirit" (CCC 1116). Also, "Holy Baptism is the basis of the whole Christian life…the gateway to life in the Spirit" (CCC 1213), and baptism "is also called '*the washing of regeneration and renewal by the Holy Spirit*' for it signifies and actually brings about the birth of water and the Spirit" (CCC 1215). What we receive in baptism, confirmation, and the Eucharist (the sacraments of Christian initiation) is awakened, enlivened, reactivated, or rekindled through the baptism in the Holy Spirit. The life we received from God at our baptism surges and flows anew as a result of new immersions into God's ongoing, merciful love.

This renewal in the life of the Holy Spirit gives us new eyes to see God and new ears to hear God's Word. It also gives many a new willingness to renounce sin and be faithful to the Gospel.

"Do not be conformed to this world, but be transformed by the renewing of your minds. So that you may discern what is the will of God, what is good and acceptable and perfect" (Romans 12:2).

NEW LIFE, NEW JOY

Pope St. John Paul II (1920–2005) spoke about this invitation to a new life as an immersion into God's very being:

> The Church professes and proclaims conversion. Conversion to God always consists in discovering His mercy, that is, in discovering that love which is patient and kind (cf. 1 Corinthians 13:4) as only the Creator and Father can be; the love to which the "God and Father of our Lord Jesus Christ" (2 Corinthians 1:3) is faithful…even to the cross and to the death and resurrection of the Son. Conversion to God is always the fruit of the "rediscovery" of this Father, who is rich in mercy.[3]

This work in our hearts is the foundation for both returning to God in the sacrament of reconciliation and acknowledging our faults to one another. After his conversion, Tony visited his sister's daughter, Peggy, who had married a black man fifteen years earlier. "Please forgive me for not loving you and your husband the way I should have," he told her. "I realize that I don't want to be like that anymore."

Baptism in the Spirit also points to the sacrament of confirmation as a personal Pentecost, which "increases the gifts [charisms and fruits] of the Holy Spirit in us…[and] gives us a special strength of the Holy Spirit" (CCC 1303). If someone were to ask you, "Did your confirmation make a difference? Have you really received the Spirit?" what would your answer be?

Therese remembers turning to another young teenager after her confirmation and asking him, "So, did anything happen?" He shrugged his shoulders and said, "No." Many years later, Therese attended a Catholic Charismatic Day of Renewal in Williamston, Michigan. After receiving prayer, her friend Irene asked, "Did anything happen?" Therese simply laughed with joy. In fact, she and Irene laughed together for almost two hours. Something *had* happened, an indescribable new beginning.

POWER TO SERVE

Baptism in the Spirit is not a new sacrament but the quickening of an earlier gift of faith. It is a participation both in the baptism of Jesus and in the events of Pentecost in the early Church. The sending of the Spirit is a vital key to the Christian life. With this key, you can be like Jesus and like St. Peter, who went from denying Jesus to boldly proclaiming him on Pentecost Sunday.

The fire of the Spirit can grow from a microscopic ember into a blazing sun. So ask yourself, "Have I accepted and received the Spirit of self-surrender and power that was evident in Jesus at the Jordan and among the disciples after Pentecost?"

St. Luke reminds us, "God anointed Jesus of Nazareth with the Holy Spirit and with power" (Acts 10:38). In the waters of the River Jordan, Jesus accepted a new outpouring of the Spirit along with the blessings of the Father. The Spirit drove him to a retreat in the desert. Then Jesus began his ministry with a proclamation in the synagogue at Nazareth: "The Spirit of the Lord is upon me" (Luke 4:18, quoting Isaiah 61:1). Gifts of teaching, healing, prayer, and deliverance from evil characterized his ministry, as he received ongoing outpourings of the Spirit.

Before the Resurrection, the disciples stood beside lepers made clean by Jesus. They knew blind and lame men and women who were made whole by the touch of Jesus. But after Pentecost, those disciples moved from being attentive yet bewildered bystanders to being a community of deliberate and unshakable witnesses to Jesus. A mighty wind rushed into their lives, spreading the consuming, purifying fire of the Spirit of Jesus and transforming them at the core of their beings.

> Now when [the Jews] saw the boldness of Peter and John and realized that they were uneducated and ordinary men, they were amazed and recognized them as companions of Jesus. (Acts 4:13)

> So if anyone is in Christ, there is a new creation: everything old has passed away; see, everything has become new! (2 Corinthians 5:17)

God offers us a transformation like those of Jesus's disciples. Like the events of Jesus's baptism and those of Pentecost, baptism in the Spirit is a conscious experience of the power of the Spirit, a new inner awareness that activates what is already deep within us, giving our spiritual lives a new dimension. Even if we are already familiar with God's voice, we can hear the Lord more clearly in our hearts.

The release of the Holy Spirit means more of God's life—but not "more" in the quantitative sense. We aren't adding something extra. Baptism in the Spirit is the release of a person who was all cramped up in a tiny space within our souls. Surrender to the Father, Son, and Spirit becomes more conscious. We move from being like seedlings to being like plants budding with magnificent blossoms. The Spirit transforms our substance, making us fresh and vibrant.

Fr. Killian (Richard) Loch, OSB, a former member of the

National Service Committee of the Catholic Charismatic Renewal, presented a workshop describing the effects of new life in the Spirit in this way: Some of us were like people hiding in submarines, raising a spiritual periscope once in a while to see if faith and worship were safe. Others were like people in rowboats trying to create lasting spiritual happiness on our own. Still others were like tugboats, exerting ourselves to drag family members to God. But now we are all sailboats, free to catch the wind of the Holy Spirit.

Alicia is an example of the transformation the Spirit effects. She struggled with alcohol and sex addictions, believing that all of her problems were someone else's fault, her parents' fault, even God's fault. She often prayed, "If you really loved me, Jesus, you would take away all my addictions. But you don't! So we are through!"

One day a friend brought Alicia to a prayer meeting, where she forgave her parents for being alcoholics. Through prayers for baptism in the Spirit and through the sacrament of penance, eventually Alicia was free to sort out all the consequences of her behavior and experience new healing, joy, sobriety, chastity, and daily strength.

Tongues, Prophecy, and Other Charisms

The Person of the Spirit is made manifest and visible through charisms, which are freely bestowed gifts and graces given to the body of Christ in service to the world. Receiving the Spirit requires openness to these charisms—gifts such as prophecy, healing, and praying in tongues.

The charisms were evident at Pentecost, when the disciples shared their faith and "began to speak in other languages, as the Spirit gave them ability" (Acts 2:4). St Paul lists some charisms in 1 Corinthians 12:4–11. Throughout the New

Testament, we see the operation of wisdom, healing, miracles, prophecy, discernment, encouragement, almsgiving, administration, faith, craftsmanship, knowledge, pastoring, mercy, and praying in tongues for the building up of the body of Christ and the evangelization of all peoples.

The Spirit uses these charisms to gather, to sanctify, and to bring new life. The *Catechism* states:

> Charisms are to be accepted with gratitude by the person who receives them and by all members of the Church as well. They are a wonderfully rich grace for the apostolic vitality and for the holiness of the entire Body of Christ, provided they really are genuine gifts of the Holy Spirit. (CCC 800)

Praying and singing in tongues are often the most noticeable manifestations of the Spirit at a charismatic gathering. The charism of tongues is a special language of non-rational prayer and song, also called *glossolalia* (Greek). Cornelius and his household experienced the gift of tongues during their conversion in Acts 10:44–48. In the Middle Ages, a similar kind of prayer was called *jubilatio* (Latin). For more about the history of this gift, see *Sounds of Wonder* by Deacon Eddie Ensley, listed in our Resource Section.

Praying in tongues is a way of surrendering voice and thoughts to God. Usually one prays or sings in an unknown language. But at times the tongue is identified by someone else. A college professor who came to one charismatic gathering asked John where he learned the Hail Mary in an old form of Middle French. John cannot even speak modern French fluently, but that night he was worshipping God in an ancient dialect.

Therese prayed in tongues while watching the attack on the

World Trade Center on September 11, 2001. For her, it was the only kind of prayer that could lift up such an unspeakable horror to God. Yet her first experience of this gift was somewhat reluctant.

Many years ago, when charismatic gifts were still a recent rediscovery in the Catholic Church, she and several friends were enjoying an Antioch Weekend retreat. Neither Therese nor the retreat leaders were convinced about the value of praying in tongues, so they weren't promoting such prayer. Then, on the Saturday afternoon of this retreat, the phone rang. "Guess what!" a fellow retreatant told Therese. "I got the gift of tongues!!"

Therese encouraged the caller but was not about to embrace this strange charism. Then came a second call and a third, from retreatants who had not even talked to each other.

"That's it!" Therese told God. "I may be stubborn, but I am not stupid. If one more person calls, then I will surrender to *any* and all charisms, including tongues." The words had hardly left her lips when, ring, "Guess what!"

So the next night, Therese went out to the barn in her back yard and prayed for the gift of tongues. She slowly made her way through all the psalms. Nothing! Then a whole rosary. Nothing! Then finally, about 3:00 AM, she heard some clear words from God: "Therese, go to bed!" It was not until two weeks later, while praying for a sick friend, that she received the gift of praying in tongues.

The charism of prophecy involves sharing a message from God. A person speaks words that he or she believes to be prompted by the Spirit. A message might be, "My children. Open your eyes to my presence. I am beside you, longing for an important place in your life and in your heart. Surrender to my love."

A companion gift to prophecy is discernment. This gift of the Spirit helps the community recognize elements of a prophetic message that are from God. For more about this gift, see the leaflet "Understanding and Exercising the Gift of Prophecy," by Chuck Hornsby.[4]

It bears emphasizing that a true prophecy *never contradicts* Scripture, Tradition, or Church teaching, because God's Spirit is not self-contradictory. Rather, sound prophecy reinforces these by providing an application of God's truth to our daily lives. For instance, a prophecy on the primacy of love might help an overly rigid prayer group pay more attention to prayer, relationships, and evangelization.

God can touch us verbally through prophecy, Scripture, inspired songs, and stories of God's action today (witness stories or testimonies). The Spirit manifests himself physically, granting a new freedom through praise and movement, such as the raising of hands. The Spirit can also enliven us visually through dreams, visions, healing of memories, and even the sight of fellow believers.

The charism of healing, which may involve the laying on of hands in prayer, is an obvious gift to the Church. In addition, charisms like administration, mercy, and teaching can infuse our actions with the fire and breath of God's Spirit, yielding more orderly relationships and greater clarity in our service to others. The list of charisms is almost endless.[5]

WHY BE CHARISMATIC?

The baptism in the Spirit is a means of embracing the fullness of Christian initiation and all that this ongoing new beginning means. The Spirit gives us the power to move forward with his gifts and bring peace and hope to our troubled world. We give flesh to God's Good News.

Part of the Good News is that God is always willing to break into history and to address our deepest hungers. The Spirit offers help for believers; invitations to faith in Christ for nonbelievers; and course corrections for our world. Charismatic renewal is one of those interventions, empowering individuals and communities to believe and to live the teachings of the Catholic faith with all the resources of the Holy Spirit:

• We can discover God's personal covenant love, which comes to us by way of the Hebrew people. We can truly say, "We are his people, and the sheep of his pasture" (Psalm 100:3).

• We can acknowledge Jesus Christ as Lord, Redeemer, Savior, and Shepherd, who came to carry our burdens and repair our broken relationships with the Father and with each other. We can find the Christ who speaks, who heals, and who teaches.

• We can immerse ourselves in the life, death, and resurrection of Jesus lived out in his body, the Church. We can enter fully into the liturgical cycles of Advent, Christmas, Lent, Easter, Pentecost, and ordinary time.

• We can expect an unending outpouring of the Holy Spirit, helping us turn from sin and self-centeredness toward God and even working miracles on our behalf. Through the Charismatic Renewal and other renewal movements, God breathes new life into the Church and the world, person by person.

God's Spirit breathes forgiveness and refocuses our hearts. Mary Anne aborted her first daughter because developing a career as a lawyer was her first priority. Later she experienced long bouts of depression. Then one day, a sick friend asked her to take him to a charismatic healing Mass. As Mary Anne prayed in the silence of Communion time, someone shared a prophetic message inviting anyone who'd had an abortion to seek God's forgiveness and healing. She turned to the Lord and wept for her unborn child.

Later in the evening, Mary Anne signed up for a New Life in the Spirit Seminar. She went to confession and experienced baptism in the Holy Spirit. The burden of remorse and guilt left her. She's now a new person in Jesus Christ, through the power of the Holy Spirit.

God's Spirit immerses us in self-giving love, into the life of the Trinity. He also empowers us to share this merciful love within the Christian community and beyond. Roger and Joyce experienced the release of the Spirit at a small faith-sharing group in their parish. They thrived on the love of this community and grew in a desire to share their lives in Jesus Christ with others. When their pastor asked them to start an evangelization committee, they jumped at the chance.

Marta offers an example of new life in the Spirit lived out in the marketplace. She attended a local charismatic prayer meeting to pray for a new job, and she ended up going through a seven-week New Life in the Spirit Seminar. Through the spiritual talks, the small group sharing, and the continued love and support of the prayer group, she experienced a breakthrough in her life. She went back to school and now works as an accountant in a clothing store. Marta tries to make Christ present in the mall where she works.

Many other people have experienced God's intervention in their lives. Have you? Watch for God's hand in a crisis, in an unexpected event, in the concern of a friend. These experiences might contain a hint of God's voice.

You too have a "salvation history"—a plan that God sets before you, so that you will be equipped to live life in the fullness of his love. God cares about you. God knows you personally and will never abandon you. Every breath that you take is a new gift from God. And God offers more than you can imagine through the presence of his Holy Spirit.

STOP AND PRAY

At Easter and Pentecost, we recommit ourselves to the Father, Son, and Holy Spirit. We remember our baptismal vows to love the Trinity. But who is this Holy Spirit? Who is this giver of gifts, graces, and charisms, especially in our everyday life?

Here are some names for the Holy Spirit from Scripture and Church teaching. Circle four that you find most meaningful.

Advocate + Comforter + Mighty Wind + Willing Spirit + Water of Life + Gift of God + Healer + Breath of God + The Presence + River of God + Consuming Fire + Soul of the Church + Power of the Most High + Lord + Glory of God + Breath of Heaven + Helper + Living Flame of Love + Counselor+ Paraclete + Dove + Giver of Gifts + Spirit of Jesus + Teacher + Holy Ghost + Anointing + Consoler + Light + Giver of Life + Spirit of Truth + Spirit of Wisdom + Spirit of the Father + Sanctifier + Holy One + Spirit of Understanding + Eternal Spirit + Strength of God + Voice of the Lord

Imagine yourself at the first Pentecost, when the Holy Spirit came down upon the praying disciples of Jesus and transformed them (see Acts 2). You might pray with hands outstretched, inviting the Spirit to fill you. Call out to him by inserting the titles you have chosen into this prayer:

Come, _____, fill my heart.
Come, _____, fill my life.
Come, _____, bless my family.
Come, _____, transform me.
End by slowly praying the Sign of the Cross.[6]

Part Two

THE CATHOLIC CHARISMATIC RENEWAL:
FIFTY YEARS WORTH CELEBRATING

Now that we have explored the work of the Holy Spirit, we hope you will join us in considering this fiftieth anniversary of the Catholic Charismatic Renewal as a true jubilee year, a time of refreshment and an opportunity for new insights. "You shall hallow the fiftieth year and you shall proclaim liberty throughout the land to all its inhabitants.... For it is a jubilee; it shall be holy to you" (Leviticus 25:10, 12).

Our point of reference is Pentecost and the rush of God's Spirit on the disciples in Acts 2:1–21. But there are many more Pentecosts in the book of Acts. After Peter and John were told not to preach, the disciples assembled and prayed for holy boldness as they renewed their commitment to God. Then "the place in which they were gathered together was shaken; and they were all filled with the Holy Spirit" (Acts 4:23–31). Later came Paul's conversion (Acts 9:1–9). Then there was the outpouring of the Spirit at the house of Cornelius, a Gentile. "While Peter was still speaking, the Holy Spirit fell upon all who heard the word.... [And] they heard them speaking in tongues and extolling God" (Acts 10:44, 46).

These manifestations fulfilled St. John the Baptist's promise of a new immersion in the Spirit for followers of Jesus Christ: "I baptize you with water for repentance, but one who is more powerful than I is coming after me.... He will baptize you with the Holy Spirit and fire" (Matthew 3:11; see Mark 1:7–8; Luke 3:16; John 1:33). Jesus expanded on this promise before his ascension into heaven: "And see, I am sending upon you what my Father promised; so stay here in the city until you have been clothed with power from on high" (Luke 24:49).

The Spirit through the Centuries

Outpourings of the Spirit have continued throughout Church history. These outpourings are part of the dynamic reality of salvation history, which climaxed in the birth, death, and resurrection of Jesus but also moves forward through God's visible and invisible interventions. Over and over again, God has met human needs with fresh manifestations of his Holy Spirit.

Studies summarized in the groundbreaking book *Fanning the Flame: What Does Baptism in the Holy Spirit Have to Do with Christian Initiation?* found that the experience of baptism in the Holy Spirit, accompanied by a full range of charisms, was a normal part of initiation in the first eight centuries of the Church. This study rediscovered doctors of the Church, such as Sts. Hilary of Poitiers (c. 315–367) and Cyril of Jerusalem (c. 315–356), who spoke about the release of the Spirit as an integral part of the liturgy and public life of the early Church.

St. Hilary describes what did and can happen:

> We who have been reborn through the sacrament of baptism experience intense joy...when we feel within us the first stirring of the Holy Spirit.... We begin to have insight into the mysteries of faith, we are able to prophesy and to speak with wisdom. We become steadfast in hope and receive the gifts of healing.[7]

The fourth century also gave rise to the monastic movement. Then, in the Middle Ages, preachers like St. Francis of Assisi (1182–1226) and St. Dominic (1170–1221), as well as prophetic mystics like St. Catherine of Siena (1347–1380), initiated the renewal of Church life.

The parade of canonized, charismatic saints continues with

St. Ignatius of Loyola (1491–1556), who took the motto "For the greater glory óf God." He once said, "Man was created to praise, do reverence to and serve God our Lord and thereby save his soul." St. Ignatius developed his Spiritual Exercises to help connect the events in Christ's life with the use of charisms in service to God and others.

The Chablais region of France experienced renewal in the 1600s, especially through the preaching and teaching of St. Francis de Sales. This movement of the Holy Spirit "ushered in a tidal wave of spiritual, evangelical, and pastoral reforms and innovations."[8] It also prompted lay and religious missionaries to journey to Quebec and even influenced the Second Vatican Council, as we will read in the next section.

Charismatic Renewal Arrives

The late nineteenth and twentieth centuries were a time of widespread renewal in the Church. Some of its highlights include Pope Leo XIII's encyclical about the Spirit, *Divinum Illud Munus* (1897), and the witness of Blessed Elena Guerra (1835–1914), who called for an intensified devotion to the Holy Spirit on New Year's Eve, 1900.

At the historic convocation of Vatican II (1962–1965), the opening prayer began with an invocation of the Holy Spirit: "We are here before You, O Holy Spirit.... Come and abide with us. Deign to penetrate our hearts. Be the guide of our actions, indicate the path we should take, and show us what we must do so that, with Your help, our work may be in all things pleasing to You."[9] And God answered. The council unleashed waves of liturgical reform and greater interest in prayer, Scripture, and ecumenism.

On the heels of the council, the charismatic movement arose to take on a significant role in the Church's mission. It began in

1967, a time of civil unrest in the United States, particularly on college campuses and in inner city ghettoes. Vietnam demonstrations, civil rights protests, and racial riots were regular features on the evening news. Then there was the unspeakable demoralization that followed the assassinations of President John F. Kennedy, Dr. Martin Luther King, Jr., and presidential candidate Robert F. Kennedy.

One part of God's merciful response to the world's woes at this time was to touch a small group of college students at Duquesne University in Pittsburgh, Pennsylvania. In February 1967, these students, some of who had already embraced the underpinnings of the Gospel message through the Cursillo movement, gathered for a weekend retreat on the Holy Spirit. Their intent was to prayerfully consider Scriptures like the Acts of the Apostles, the witness of a few Protestant Pentecostal friends, and a book called *The Cross and the Switchblade* by David Wilkerson.

As the retreat progressed, God stepped in and granted the spontaneous release of the Holy Spirit to about half of the participants. Patti Gallagher Mansfield describes the experiences of renewal and empowerment that began with that retreat in her recently revised book *As by a New Pentecost*. When the students returned to Duquesne,

> "We were like [people] dreaming. Then our mouth was filled with laughter; and our tongue with rejoicing" (Psalm 126).... A friend asked me what had come over me. "If I didn't know you better, Patti, I'd say you were drunk!" he exclaimed. Of course, I was quick to point out to him that this was *the very thing* said of the apostles after Pentecost (Acts 2:13).... Yes, I was drunk, but not on wine![10]

After the retreat, these young people contacted retreat leaders and campus ministry efforts all over the country. Their goal was to inspire faith, pray with others, share the Gospel message, and highlight the role of the Spirit. Theirs was more than just a contagious idealism. In 1973, thirty-five thousand Catholics of all ages gathered for a national conference at Notre Dame University—both to celebrate the Spirit and to seek his strength and empowerment as Jesus's followers.

John recalls the long bus ride from Massachusetts to Indiana for this 1973 conference. It seemed even longer because of a full-blown case of the flu, which worsened as the miles went by. This illness, in addition to a serious thyroid problem, rendered him seriously miserable and almost immobile. When the bus arrived at Notre Dame, John wanted to kiss the ground. Finally, he thought, he could be sick in a bed.

Instead, someone whisked John off to a small Mass with pilgrims from another state. As he received the Eucharist, he was healed. No more flu and no more thyroid problems. In fact, two weeks later, several medical tests rendered his doctor speechless.

The next twenty years brought more regional, national, and international conferences. Scholarly research, begun by Cardinal Leo J. Suenens of Belgium, affirmed the charismatic roots of the Catholic Church and asserted that the power of the Holy Spirit is integral to our tradition as Catholics, not peripheral to it. It is part of our personal and communal heritage, to be continuously manifested in a variety of charisms.

The Catholic Charismatic Renewal has had global impact. For example, the Renewal in Brazil was featured in *Time* magazine in 2007. The Church in Brazil had experienced a tremendous exodus of Catholics, especially young people, from the practice of their faith. Now hundreds of covenant communities (see Glossary) were developing, as well as numerous television and radio programs that inspire believers. *Time* noted:

> The best example of the trend is Fr. Marcelo Rossi, a charismatic and media-savvy priest who has sold millions of CDs featuring songs like "Clapping for Jesus," "Raise Your Hands" and the "Jesus Twist." Rossi has a daily radio show, two weekly TV shows and a busy web portal, and he hosts regular concerts-cum-shows at which thousands of young fans dance to his catchy Gospel pop. He once attracted 2.4 million fans to an appearance in Sao Paulo, and his draw is such that he has been invited to give a live performance immediately after Benedict XVI says Mass in Sao Paulo.[11]

What Do the Popes Think of the Charismatic Renewal?
Connecting to the larger institutional Church has always been important to members and groups in the Catholic Charismatic Renewal. This was especially important in the earliest decade of the Renewal, since many of the movement's first mentors were from Pentecostal churches. Catholic participants reexamined Vatican II documents for clues about the foundation upon which this renewal stood. They reflected on Pope St. John XXIII's prayer for a New Pentecost, which he offered for the success of the council:

> Renew [your] wonders in this our day, as by a new Pentecost. Grant to [your] Church that, being of one mind and steadfast in prayer with Mary, the Mother of Jesus, and following the lead of blessed Peter, it may advance the reign of our Divine Savior, the reign of truth and justice, the reign of love and peace. Amen.[12]

Renewal leaders looked at Vatican II's Decree on the Apostolate of Lay People in a fresh light, especially as it describes the presence of the Spirit and the role of charisms:

> The Holy Spirit...gives the faithful special gifts.... From the reception of these charisms...there arises for each of the faithful the right and duty of exercising them in the Church and in the world for the good of men...of exercising them in the freedom of the Holy Spirit who "breathes where he wills" (John 3:8)....[13]

In 1975, ten thousand people from all over the world gathered in Rome for the ninth international conference on the Renewal. Blessed Pope Paul VI's words were a source of affirmation as well as direction and discernment.

> The Church and the world need more than ever that "the miracle of Pentecost should continue in history." ...Nothing is more necessary to this increasingly secularized world than the witness of this "spiritual renewal" that we see the Holy Spirit evoking.... How could this "spiritual renewal" not be "good fortune" for the Church and the world?[14]

A decade later, Pope St. John Paul II appointed Archbishop Paul Josef Cordes, of the Pontifical Council for the Laity, to be a guide to the Charismatic Renewal in the Church. In that capacity, Archbishop Cordes addressed the Silver Anniversary Conference on the Catholic Charismatic Renewal, at Pittsburgh in 1992, with "The Call to the Catholic Charismatic Renewal from the Church Universal." He issued two challenges. The first was to foster a greater understanding and renewal of the sacraments of Christian initiation (baptism, confirmation, and the Eucharist), "so that all God's people may one day experience a greater fullness of life in Christ by being—as you call it—baptized in the Spirit."[15]

The second challenge was to embrace the Church's mission of evangelization. We are to be missionaries grounded in love for Christ, worship of the Father, and empowerment by the Holy Spirit. Quoting Pope St. John Paul II, Archbishop Cordes said, "Your contribution to the re-evangelization of society will be made in the first place by *personal witness to the indwelling Spirit and by showing forth His presence through works of holiness and solidarity.*"[16]

Pope Benedict XVI went a step further in affirming the role of charisms as we live our baptismal faith in daily life. During an address to charismatic leaders in 2008, he said:

> Charism, which appeared as visible signs of the coming of the Holy Spirit, is not a historical event of the past, but a reality ever alive. It is the same divine Spirit, soul of the Church, that acts in every age, and those mysterious and effective interventions of the Spirit are manifest in our time in a providential way.... We can, therefore, rightly say that one of the positive elements and aspects of the Community of the Catholic Charismatic Renewal is precisely their emphasis on the charisms or gifts of the Holy Spirit.[17]

Pope Francis embraced Charismatic Renewal as early as 1999, when he began to celebrate Masses and teach in the annual school of formation for Catholic charismatics in Argentina. Austen Ivereigh reports that later, in 2006, then-Cardinal Bergoglio shocked many by kneeling on the stage for prayer at a large charismatic gathering in the Buenos Aires stadium.[18] A few months before the 2013 conclave, the Argentinian Episcopal Conference appointed Cardinal Bergoglio as spiritual assistant of the Charismatic Renewal in that country. And after the final count electing him pope, he took his overwhelming and fearsome sense of responsibility to prayer in a small chapel.

> My head was completely empty, and I was seized by a great anxiety. To make it go away and relax, I closed my eyes and made every thought disappear.... I no longer had any anxiety or emotion. At a certain point, I was filled with a great light. It lasted a moment, but to me it seemed very long.[19]

Addressing the Renewal in the Spirit Conference in Rome on June 1, 2014, the pope counseled:

> Brothers and sisters, remember: adore the Lord God: this is the foundation! To adore God. Seek sanctity in the new life of the Holy Spirit. Be dispensers of the grace of God. Avoid the danger of excessive organization.
>
> Go out into the streets to evangelize, proclaiming the Gospel. Remember that the Church was born "in going forth" that Pentecost morning. Be close to the poor and touch in their flesh the wounded flesh of Jesus. Let yourselves by led by the Holy Spirit, with that freedom and, please, do not cage the Holy Spirit! With liberty!
>
> Seek the unity of the Renewal, unity that comes from the Trinity!
>
> And I await you all, Charismatics of the world, to celebrate, together with the Pope, your Great Jubilee in Pentecost of 2017, in Saint Peter's Square! Thank you![20]

At the root of appreciating these papal statements, and answering the two challenges offered by (the now) Cardinal Cordes, is an understanding of our baptismal vows, renewed every Easter and affirmed when we pray the Nicene Creed at Mass. Both this creed and these vows ask us, "Do I choose the Father, Son, and Spirit as the center of my life? Do I strive to live, think, and feel by the light of God's merciful presence? Do I choose the Church as my spiritual community and its past and present believers as spiritual companions and mentors?"

Fifty Years of Charismatic Renewal in the United States

God has done a great deal since the Duquesne retreat in 1967 and the 1973 national conference at Notre Dame. At the time of that conference, there were about 50,000 Catholics involved in the Renewal. By 1984, there were about 5,700 prayer groups with a weekly attendance of over 250,000 people, as well as covenant communities (both Catholic and ecumenical) in about a hundred locations and many healing services throughout the country.

The spread of prayer groups in the first decades of the Renewal brought forth several spiritual phenomena. The first was spontaneous group prayer, which became the context for praying in tongues and for gestures like raising one's arms to God. The second was meditation on Scripture passages and their prophetic meaning, a form of *lectio divina*, Latin for "sacred reading." The third was individual prayer for healing and other needs, through the laying on of hands and group intercessory prayer. The fourth was inspired teaching, to advance the faith formation of those present.

Even now, we see these phenomena filtering into faith-sharing groups and parish ministries. One of the goals of the Charismatic Renewal is to bring its best, its spiritual riches, to the whole Church.

During the most recent two decades of the Catholic Charismatic Renewal, there has been a decrease in numbers of English-speaking prayer groups in the United States but an increase in charismatically inspired ministry groups, centers, religious orders, diocesan charismatic offices, and lay associations. Here are just a few of the latter: Life Teen, LAMP Catholic Ministries, Magnificat, FOCUS (Fellowship of Catholic University Students), NET Ministries, the Sword of the Spirit, Renewal Ministries, the People of Praise, and the Fraternity of Priests. These ministries can be called "streams of the renewal." The Holy Spirit is never limited to one expression of grace-filled discipleship.

The United States Conference of Catholic Bishops has offered guidance to the Charismatic Renewal through several positive statements (in 1969, 1975, 1984, and 1997). The most recent document, "Grace for the New Springtime," states:

> Our Ad Hoc Committee for the Catholic Charismatic Renewal felt it was appropriate to issue a statement of affirmation, support and encouragement to those who have experienced the release of gifts and charisms of the Holy Spirit—known as baptism in the Holy Spirit (Acts 1:4).
>
> …We desire to affirm the positive impact this move of the Spirit has had in the lives of millions of people and through them the life of the Church.
>
> …We, likewise, "encourage them in their efforts to renew the life of the Church."[21]

The bishops quote their 1984 document: "Insofar as the Renewal makes its own what is central to the enduring reality of the Gospel, it cannot be dismissed as peripheral to the life of the Church." And then they cite Pope St. John Paul II's description (speaking in 1979) of the Charismatic Renewal as "a sign of the Spirit's action…(and) a very important component in the total renewal of the Church."[22]

Thus:

> It is our conviction that baptism in the Holy Spirit, understood as the reawakening in Christian experience of the presence and action of the Holy Spirit given in Christian initiation, and manifested in a broad range of charisms, including those closely associated with the Catholic Charismatic Renewal, is part of the normal Christian life.[23]

Tasks for the Charismatic Renewal

Human beings are interested in several kinds of power: purchasing power; computing power; and even the emotional and psychological strength to face obstacles in life. Jesus, on the other hand, invites us to seek a much more profound strength and power: an ongoing, personal encounter with the Holy Spirit. He offers an invitation to the entire body of Christ. Blessed Pope Paul VI put it this way: "What is the primary and ultimate need of our beloved and holy Church?... This need is the Spirit.... [T]he Church needs her eternal Pentecost; she needs fire in her heart, words on her lips, a glance that is prophetic."[24]

On the threshold of the golden jubilee of the Catholic Charismatic Renewal, Pope Francis spoke about this renewal as "a current of grace."[25] This is the ultimate reality of what has happened and will continue to happen. But when God mixes with humanity, there is also a paradox. There is both a current of grace and the sociological reality of an organized movement. We move forward keeping both these in mind.

One task of the Renewal is to appreciate its prophetic identity as an ecclesial movement alongside other currents of grace in the Catholic Church. Some of these are Cursillo, Christian Life Communities, the Christian Family Movement, Focolare,

Neocatechumenal Way, Marriage Encounter, and L'Arche. It is important to humbly promote the Charismatic Renewal's unique identity, centered on fostering the grace of baptism in the Holy Spirit and openness to charisms, in the context of the whole Catholic Church as we all serve the global human community.

This particular identity must also be constantly focused and refocused in the steadfast proclamation that "Jesus is Lord." All of us who are renewed in the Spirit must seek the grace to live and share the Good News of Jesus Christ, as emphasized by Pope Francis: "Jesus Christ loves you; he gave his life to save you; and now he is living at your side every day to enlighten, strengthen and free you."[26]

The Catholic Charismatic Renewal accomplishes this by promoting baptism in the Holy Spirit as "a life-transforming experience of the love of God the Father poured into one's heart by the Holy Spirit, received through a surrender to the lordship of Jesus Christ."[27] We are called to a daily, radical obedience to the Holy Spirit through personal and communal prayer; the reading and study of Scripture, Church teaching, and Tradition; as well as the exercise of the full spectrum of the charisms of the Spirit. Surrendering to the movements of the Holy Spirit among us, we realize, in the words of Pope Francis, "a renewing breath of the Spirit for all the members of the Church, laity, religious, priests and bishops. It is a challenge for us all. One does not form part of the Renewal, rather, the Renewal becomes a part of us provided that we accept the grace it offers us."[28]

The second focus espoused by the leaders of the Charismatic Renewal is a call to build Christ-centered unity among the various streams within the Renewal. These include ethnic groups, ministries, associations, covenant communities, organizations, institutes, religious orders, and parishes, which together witness in word and deed to a renewed, Spirit-filled life in the Catholic Church. This unity is based on our communion with charismatic men and women through the centuries, like Blessed Elena Guerra and Pope Leo XIII. We also share a spiritual heritage with those who welcomed the outpouring of the Spirit through the Azusa Street Revival of 1906 through 1915, with classical Pentecostal churches dating from 1900 to the present, and with mainline Protestant neo-Pentecostals originating in the 1950s and 1960s.

Pope Francis summarizes this second focus on unity:

> We are speaking of the work of the Holy Spirit, not our own. Unity in the diversity of expressions of reality, as many as the Holy Spirit wills to arouse. It is also necessary to remember that the whole, namely, this unity, is greater than the part, and the part cannot attribute the whole to itself. For instance, one cannot say: "We are the current called Catholic Charismatic Renewal and you are not." This cannot be said…it does not come from the Spirit; the Holy Spirit breathes where he wills, when he will and as he wills. Unity in diversity and in the truth that is Jesus himself….[29]

Stop and Pray

We encourage you to take stock of your response to what God has been doing among his people. If you are baptized into the body of Christ, perhaps God is offering you an even more radical discipleship. If you have not been baptized, perhaps God is calling you to make your home within the Catholic Church. Either way, we urge you to welcome the Holy Spirit and his gifts with this prayer:

> Jesus, I know now that I am yours and you are mine forever.

I thank you for sending your Spirit to me,
that I might have the power to live this new life with
you.
Stir up your Spirit in me.
Release your Spirit in me.
Baptize me with the fullness of your Spirit,
that I may experience your presence and power in my
life,
that I may find new meaning in your Scriptures,
that I may find new meaning in the sacraments,
that I may find delight and comfort in prayer,
that I may be able to love as you love and forgive as
you forgive,
that I may discover and use the gifts you give me for
the life of the Church,
that I may experience the peace and the joy that you
have promised.
Fill me with your Spirit, Jesus.
I wish to receive all that you have to give me. Amen.[30]

The Church's primary mission is to evangelize (see CCC 848–856, 858). When we use the gifts and tools of the Holy Spirit to bring others to Jesus, the whole Church flourishes. In *The Joy of the Gospel*, Pope Francis speaks about this purpose:

> Every Christian is challenged, here and now, to be actively engaged in evangelization.... Every Christian is a missionary to the extent that he or she has encountered the love of God in Christ Jesus: we no longer say that we are "disciples" and "missionaries," but rather that we are always "missionary disciples."[31]

Jesus promised his disciples (and us), "[You] will receive power when the Holy Spirit has come upon you," and then directed how to use that power: "You will be my witnesses...to the ends of the earth" (Acts 1:8).

"What does this call to power and to witness have to do with me?" you might ask. Answering this question involves decisions about faith and discipleship in daily life. What connections do you make between your daily life and your faith?

The Gospel is the Good News of new life and salvation given to us by God. When we make this message a part of our souls, through the intervention of the Holy Spirit, we are ready for ministry, as Jesus demonstrated after his baptism in the Jordan. And it is the power of the Holy Spirit, at work in each of us and in the life of the Church, that makes this possible. Through the Holy Spirit, the Soul of the Church, we can together give witness to all of the Good News again and again.

Dancing with the Maker of the Stars

Think about a time when you asked for God's help. Perhaps it was a time of sickness, loneliness, death, or confusion— yesterday or forty years ago. What happened when you reached out to God? How did you feel about God as a result of your experience? What conclusions did you reach about God's presence?

How does God act in your day? Have you known the healing touch of Jesus? Have you challenged yourself to uncover the rich meanings of the creeds, doctrines, and teachings of the Church? Are you aware of God's ongoing invitation to an inti- mate and communal encounter with the Father, Son, and Holy Spirit? Jesus is offering you this gift right now!

Think of your spiritual life as a three-step waltz with God. The steps are *death, resurrection,* and *new life.* The Holy Spirit is the beat, and Jesus is your partner. *Die* (with Christ). *Rise* (as God lifts you up). *Reign* (daily) through a life overflowing with charisms, fruits, and blessings. Then let the waltz start all over again, spiraling on in some new corner of your soul, in response to a new tragedy or a joy that engulfs you. Let the Trinity sweep you off your feet and draw you into eternal life, again and again.

> The One whom the Father has sent into our hearts, the Spirit of his Son, is truly God.... The Spirit is inseparable from [the Father and the Son].... When the Father sends his Word, he always sends his Breath. In their joint mission, the Son and the Holy Spirit are distinct but inseparable. To be sure, it is Christ who is seen, the visible image of the invisible God, but it is the Spirit who reveals him. (*CCC,* 689; see Galatians 4:6)

Review the images you chose for the Holy Spirit at the end of part one. In order to know the release of the Spirit and the waltz of the spiritual life, you must be willing to adopt an ever-expanding vision of the work of God's Spirit. On one end of the spectrum is Elijah the prophet, who experienced the Spirit as "a sound of sheer silence" (1 Kings 19:12). Have you? Are you *willing* to listen for the Holy Spirit?

On the other end is the community of the apostles, who together experienced the dynamic fire of the Spirit rushing upon them at Pentecost. Are you willing to share your faith experiences with others, within and beyond the body of Christ?

John's Gospel describes the Spirit as living water, as the breath of Jesus, and also as the Paraclete—a kind of bodyguard and intimate companion (see John 7:38–39; 14:26; 20:22). Fr. John Haughey, an early leader in the Catholic Charismatic Renewal, offers words of encouragement as we try to follow this invisible and often elusive Person. He says that our struggle is partly based in a major characteristic of the Holy Spirit, which is a kind of transparency. "The Spirit aims at being inconspicuous. In activity it points to the Other, making us aware of Jesus as our Lord and God as our Father."[32]

We must slow down, quiet ourselves, and let the Spirit of Jesus find us. Then let God send us forth on his mission with what we have been given.

Strength for Catholic Charismatic Discipleship

The Holy Spirit continually offers fresh outpourings of strength and grace. But this life-giving strength is not just for us. The Spirit gives gifts for the sake of the many communities with whom we share our lives—family, friends, coworkers, and faith communities.

While speaking at the National Shrine in Washington, DC, Pope Francis said that each of us and all of us together are sent forth as everyday missionaries. "Mission is never the fruit of a perfectly planned program or a well-organized manual. Mission is always the fruit of a life which knows what it is to be found and healed, encountered and forgiven."[33]

So let's review what has been given to us and what we can bring to others. The word *GOSPEL* will guide us:

G is for GOD, the creator and Father of all, who loves us unconditionally and wants our happiness (see 1 John 4:7–8).

O is for OURSELVES and our situation as children who have broken our relationship with God through sin (see Genesis 1:26–27).

S is for our SAVIOR, Jesus Christ, who was sent to redeem us, heal us, reconcile us, and reunite us with the Father (see John 3:16–17;1 John 4:9–12).

P is for PENTECOST and the PROMISE of power from the Holy Spirit, who helps us turn from sin and selfishness to believe in Christ and to share our faith with others (see Luke 24:49; Acts 1:8).

E is for EVERYDAY ENTRY into new life, the decision to make Jesus the center of our personal and communal lives every day (see Acts 2:37–42; Colossians 3:1–4).

L is for the LOCAL body of Christ and for LITURGY (see Acts 2:46–47; Ephesians 3:21). The celebration and living out of the sacraments help us grow in Jesus. This includes prayer, learning, community, and service as part of the evangelizing mission of the Church.

Here is an example of one woman's awakening to the Holy Spirit. Kat, from Ireland, often prayed the rosary and attended parish missions, but she did not have a very close relationship with God. She was just going through the motions. Then one day she hit rock bottom as a result of abuse. Kat was putting clothes on the line when she stopped and cried out to God, "Are you there? Do you care about what is happening to me?" It was a cry for GOD's love and for a SAVIOR.

Kat writes that three weeks later, as she was "sitting by the fireplace and thinking about Jesus, all of a sudden a tremendous peace came over me. I knew without a doubt that God loved me. As a simple confirmation of this grace, I noticed a nearby spider, and for the first time in my life, I was not afraid, and I have not been afraid of spiders since." This was an EVERYDAY ENTRY into God's presence.

"The next morning, I went to Mass and asked Jesus to use me to help others. Then a lady sat down behind me who had an awful wheeze, so I started to pray for her. What a change! Here I was praying for someone else!" The LOCAL body of Christ became important in the context of the LITURGY. "The Holy Spirit gave me the gifts of intercessory prayer and discernment, which I have since used to help people in a variety of difficult situations."

You may find it helpful to memorize these aspects of *GOSPEL*. It will help you share the Good News with others. You might also use its individual points to assess your own encounters with God and to note which truths are in need of strengthening. You can confidently ask the Holy Spirit to solidify these truths in your mind, heart, and soul.

Becoming an Evangelizer

Let's begin with our friend Roland's witness:

> I was born into a good Catholic family and attended Mass every Sunday. It was part of my upbringing. I believed that religion was a manmade system to keep people like me from misbehavior.

Around 1970, I attended a Catholic charismatic prayer meeting. I heard witnesses of healings. Then I brought my dad for healing prayer and was moved to ask the group for prayers for my soul. Hands were laid on me as the people stormed heaven. I was over-whelmed with love. Within two weeks I was praying in tongues, and a whole new world opened up for me. I had strong desires to share my faith and couldn't say enough about Jesus. God healed my wife, my children, and me and gave me an understanding of the Catholic faith and of the Scriptures. I grew deeper in love for Jesus and in a desire to serve him, so I applied to the permanent deaconate and was ordained.

Ordination enabled me to minister in a twofold way, by word and by sacrament. First, I could proclaim the Good News of God's love in my preaching, teaching, and intercessory prayer. Second, I could administer the sacraments of baptism and marriage and give the Body of Christ to the faithful at Mass, at nursing homes, and in hospitals. Loving and serving God in his people is the most fulfilling thing I do.

Roland's story reminds us of something that Blessed Pope Paul VI said:

The person who has been evangelized goes on to evangelize others. Here lies the test of truth, the touchstone of evangelization: it is unthinkable that a person should accept the Word and give himself to the kingdom without becoming a person who bears witness to it and proclaims it in his turn.[34]

We challenge you to ask yourself, "Have I been truly evangelized? Have I accepted the proclamation of salvation in Jesus? Have I been transformed by the Good News? Has this transformation filtered into every fiber of my being, every thought and action? Am I ready to share my faith and let God's love spill out on those around me, through the charisms and fruits of the Holy Spirit that I am being given?"

The Church has a special word for all the ways we can share our faith with others. The word is *evangelization*—which means giving flesh to the message of Jesus in word and deed, knowing that the Holy Spirit will change hearts and minds in the process. Through the presence of the Father, Son, and Holy Spirit, we can move from accidental kindnesses and invisible beliefs toward intentional acts of faith as charismatic disciples who enable others to experience Jesus in new ways.

Here are four simple steps we can take to evangelize and to connect us and others to Jesus: pray, care, share, and dare to invite.[35]

• PRAY: Evangelizing, intercessory prayer is not just petitioning God for what is needed but asking God to intervene in a person's life, visualizing Jesus interacting with that someone, and developing a prayerful concern about her or his spiritual life.

• CARE: Caring is the most crucial step in connecting others to Jesus. It includes befriending someone by listening; using charisms of mercy, encouragement, and almsgiving to care for others (especially the poor); and engaging in everyday acts of love, healing, and social justice with those in need. These are the fabric of daily life and of parish ministry.

• SHARE: Choose "evangelizing conversations" that include a statement of faith, a story of God's intervention in your life, or part or all of the *GOSPEL* message. Let the charisms of discernment and kindness always temper this sharing. Remember: God is present to us in daily conversations and wants to build spiritual community among us.

• DARE TO INVITE: Evangelizing invitations include both encouraging someone toward a personal and deepening relationship with God and inviting someone into a relationship with the body of Christ. You might ask someone to join you at a Mass, a Bible study, or another parish event. Afterward, ask that person what the experience was like for him or her.

Faith communities and ministries must take these steps to evangelize together, so that God's love can be experienced within a community of caring people. You can bring an evangelizing awareness into any group with whom you serve. You can advocate for evangelizing ministry by asking, "Do we seek the Spirit's wisdom in order to connect everyone we serve with Jesus?" Fr. George Montague reminds us that ministries "will achieve God's purpose to the extent that they are fed by the worship gifts of praise, listening to the word (prophecy), and healing."[36]

Beyond the Back Yard

No matter what has already happened in your conversations with God—in your own spiritual back yard, so to speak—life in the Spirit is not just about you. Your house, your apartment, your back yard, is part of the territory of a Catholic parish, whether you have ever visited that parish or not, whether you even know its name. God has given you sisters and brothers in faith and wants to nourish you at the table of your spiritual family, despite how messy it might be. So visit, become involved, and face any problems you see head on. When St. Teresa of Calcutta (1910–1997) was asked what was wrong with the Church, her reply was, "You and me!"[37]

If and when you were baptized into the life of the Trinity, it was not as an isolated person but as a tiny organism in a larger whole. You were baptized into the richness and the foibles of God's life as it is shared in the Church, the communion of saints here on earth. It can be a mysterious paradox to be called to be a Eucharistic follower of Jesus, filled with his Holy Spirit yet intertwined with broken siblings all being consecrated by receiving the Body and Blood of Christ together.

And furthermore, the Consecration of the Eucharist begins with a prayer called the *epiclesis*, Greek for "invocation" or "calling down." The priest asks God to send the Holy Spirit down upon the gifts of bread and wine, transforming them into the Body and Blood of Jesus, the Christ. Then we too can surrender the bread of our lives and be transformed into Jesus.

At one point, our young son Charlie had difficulty with the idea of the Eucharist. "Is Jesus cut into pieces?" he wanted to know. And no answer satisfied him, so we asked Fr. Jim.

"That's easy," said the priest. "If I break a mirror into hundreds of pieces and you lean over them, how many Charlies will you see?" "Hundreds!" was Charlie's smiling reply.

We are all called to reflect Jesus through the power of the Holy Spirit. Are you ready to let God polish and deepen that reflection in your life?

Are You Willing?

At one Easter Vigil, we had some excitement kindling the Easter fire. Just as Fr. Pat reached down and ignited the flames, a stiff wind stirred those flames into a blaze that threatened his sleeve and arm. We all held our breath as he took a quick step backward. He was safe. But do we so want to be "safe" that we back away from the surprises that come with surrendering to the Holy Spirit?

Jesus Christ was sent into the world by God the Father in the power of the Holy Spirit. He became flesh and "pitched his tent" among us (John 1:14). He came as *the* Missionary— leaping across time, space, languages, age groups, and cultures to reveal God's unconditional love for us. He invites us to become missionaries by bringing God's love into our neighborhoods, communities, parishes, and workplaces. To live out this call, we need to think and act as missionaries.

How many of these statements are you willing to live out in your daily life?

_____ I sense Christ's call to make my service to others an evangelizing act of love.

_____ I am on a mission with Jesus. I am not alone. He is at my side.

_____ I look for ways God is already working in those around me, so I can thank God.

_____ I want to share the Good News of Jesus by sharing what God has done for me.

_____ I want to work on a team in the mission of evangelization.

_____ I feel strengthened and sent by my local faith community to live the Good News.

_____ I believe the Holy Spirit is working through me and through the whole body of Christ in complementary ways.

After prayerfully reviewing these, choose one that you want Jesus to help you fulfill. End with the following prayer:

> O my Lord Jesus!
> Teach me to be generous;
> teach me to serve you as you deserve,
> to give and not to count the cost,
> to toil and not to ask for rest,
> to labor, seeking no reward,
> save that of knowing that I do your will.[38]
> —St. Francis Xavier (1507–1552)

Francis MacNutt describes baptism in the Holy Spirit as an event in a person's life that brings a greater ongoing awareness of the "*presence*, the *person*, and the *power* of the Risen Christ."[39] We pray that you experience such an event often in your relationship with God and just as often in the midst of God's people, sent to serve God's world. "So if anyone is in Christ, there is a new creation: everything old has passed away; see, everything has become new! All this is from God, who reconciled us to himself through Christ" (2 Corinthians 5:17–18).

It is not easy to surrender to God's surprising gift of new life, but many have done so. The challenge is to continuously place ourselves before God, seeking more for the sake of the people in our lives. The invitation is to seek something new from Jesus every day, to embrace the Person and the gifts of the Holy Spirit.

We admire Jay, who came from an entirely unchurched family, but attended a Lutheran high school. He was later surprised, as an adult when he knelt at his grandfather's casket, to hear God say, "Isn't it time you came to me?" Jay later called his girlfriend's parish. What did this mean? What should he do next? After meeting with a pastoral associate, he decided to attend RCIA (the Rite of Christian Initiation for Adults), and several months later he was baptized and confirmed. Now Jay is married and serves as a greeter in his parish.

Our new friend Alex, a recent immigrant from Brazil, also answered God's invitation:

I was educated by my parents to live the Catholic faith through all the sacraments. And my father also taught me the duties of a man to take care of his family. But when I married, I often neglected my wife, until one day, my wife's customer saw her sadness and asked if he could pray for her. My wife said yes, but at the end of their prayers, he warned her about a former girlfriend of mine who had plans to steal me away.

I went to my mother's prayer group and experienced a special prayer for healing and deliverance. At the end, I no longer wanted to follow the old ways. I felt I had been freed from evil, and I was thirsty, hungry to know God. I wanted to speak of Jesus Christ to others, to help them find him, to follow the way of the Catholic Church.

Now I continue the purification process—searching, reading the Word of God, helping in my community. Today I know a little more of my God, tomorrow I will know a little more, and so on, because God is always with me.

WHERE CAN I FIND CHARISMATIC RENEWAL?

If new life in the Spirit and charismatic renewal are new to you, may we extend a personal invitation? Come and see what the Lord is doing at charismatic gatherings. There are many events throughout the country and the world where people gather to praise God and to support one another in the dynamic life of the Holy Spirit: prayer groups, Holy Spirit retreats, healing Masses, covenant community gatherings, New Life in the Spirit Seminars, and diocesan, regional, and national charismatic conferences. Below are some possible places where you can search for what is right for you. More information about each of these organizations is included in the Resource Section at the end of this booklet.

Explore on an international level by visiting iccrs.org. This is the website of International Catholic Charismatic Renewal Services, a worldwide resource for the Renewal. Here you will find videos, newsletters, and links to covenant communities, Renewal centers, religious communities, and ministries.

View the online video series by Fr. Dave Pivonka called *The Wild Goose,* "a work of the Holy Spirit, which is awakening in the hearts of all those participating God's love and transforming power."[40] The series includes fourteen segments about the work of the Holy Spirit, the first three of which give the foundation for the others.

Explore resources in the United States by visiting nsc-chariscenter.org. You will find a list of official liaisons to the Charismatic Renewal for the dioceses in the United States, listings for prayer groups and covenant communities, and contacts for diocesan, regional, and national ministries, conferences, and gatherings. This organization also offers a regular newsletter, leaflets, books, and a Facebook page.

Attend an introductory Holy Spirit workshop or regional retreat. These programs are designed to help participants experience the release, power, and presence of the Spirit promised and given in baptism, confirmation, and the Eucharist. One video option is *As by a New Pentecost*, which includes seven sessions with presentations and short discussions. You can purchase this at nsc-chariscenter.org.

Catholic charismatic conferences sometimes offer introductory sessions to Charismatic Renewal. For a listing of youth, young adult, and adult conferences, visit steubenvilleconferences.com.

Help from the saints is always available. Pope Benedict XVI reminds us, "To renew the church in every age, God raises up saints, who themselves have been renewed by God and are in constant contact with God."[41] This is God's preferred solution to the world's problems, since God is about relationships that draw us closer to himself and to one another. So it can be fruitful to examine the saints' lives for evidence of the dynamic use of charisms grounded in holiness and coupled with the fruits of the Spirit—"love, joy, peace, patience, kindness, generosity, faithfulness, gentleness, and self-control" (Galatians 22—23). God uses saints to propel us into everyday lives of service.

We talked about some saints of renewal in part two, such as Francis of Assisi, Ignatius of Loyola, and Catherine of Siena. Here are a few others who can inspire us in our use of charisms for the glory of God and the building of the Church.

St. Margaret Mary Alacoque (1647–1690) shared her visions of the Sacred Heart of Jesus as a springboard for promoting an awareness of God's personal love for each of us.

> Hail, Heart of my Jesus: save me!
>
> Hail, Heart of my Creator: perfect me!
>
> Hail, Heart of my Savior: deliver me!…
>
> Hail, Heart of my Master: teach me!…
>
> Hail, Heart of my Pastor: guard me!
>
> Hail, Heart of my Brother: stay with me!
>
> Hail, Heart of my Incomparable Goodness: have mercy on me!
>
> Hail, most loving Heart: inflame me. Amen.[42]

Sherry Weddell offers some lesser-known models of the dynamic use of charisms:

> Blessed Henry the Shoemaker (c. 1600–1666) is an example of the charism of Pastoring. He combined the trade of shoemaker with a deep spiritual life. Henry

prayed and fasted for the spiritual welfare of his fellow shoemakers and formed a religious association for shoemakers. The members had prayer in common, attended daily Mass, visited prisons and hospitals and made an annual retreat. Branches started up in other cities and other tradesmen started similar groups.

Venerable Henriette Delille (1813–1862) is an example of the charism of Mercy. Henriette was born in New Orleans into a free family of mixed race whose daughters were raised to be elegant mistresses of wealthy white men…. [Instead] she began helping a French nun teach the catechism to slaves. In the face of many legal and social barriers, including the opposition of her own family, Henriette founded an order of African American nuns that identified with and ministered to slaves and the black community.[43]

Pope St. John Paul II canonized 480 new saints and beatified 1,338 people, including hundreds of women and men from recent centuries, from every corner of the globe and every culture. These followers of Jesus are models for facing current challenges to faith. They can teach us much about charismatic discipleship and service.

St. Gianna Beretta Molla (1922–1962), for example, faced the sobering issue of abortion, both as a doctor and in her own pregnancy. She employed the gifts of wisdom, intercessory prayer, and discernment to make personal medical decisions, with moral and ethical consequences.

Befriend the saints, perhaps beginning with Mary, Mother of God and Spouse of the Holy Spirit. Let the saints introduce you to a life of prayer, service, charisms, and holiness. Learn about the bouquets of charisms, graces, and virtues you can offer to God.

Choose one new saintly friend who can teach you about the activity of the Holy Spirit. Let this saint help you appreciate any one charism as a tiny flower in the garden of holiness, where God invites you to dwell as a faithful disciple, serving the Father, Son, and Holy Spirit above all else. Be firm in offering your life for the sake of the Gospel. Be resolved in answering God's call to be a charismatic saint. As Pope St. John Paul II writes,

> Men and women saints have always been the source and origin of renewal in the most difficult circumstances in the Church's history. Today we have the greatest need of saints whom we must assiduously beg God to raise up.[44]

A Final Word of Encouragement

Our greatest resource is prayer. It is the 'how' and the 'where' of new life in the Spirit. God's presence is where you will find charismatic renewal. Here, God will grant you the gift of surrender to the Holy Spirit, to the Father, and to Jesus, our redeemer. Prayer is the antidote for spiritual amnesia, the means for bridging any disconnect from God's presence in the Church. Don't give up in pursuing a life of prayer and faith! God has much in store for you.

"Let us run with perseverance the race that is set before us, looking to Jesus the pioneer and perfecter of our faith" (Hebrews 12:1).

NOTES

1. John Boucher, "Come, Holy Spirit," song adapted from St. John of the Cross, "Living Flame," https://www.youtube.com/watch?v=B7FHcVCGO-A.

2. Abundant information and news about the international Charismatic Renewal is available on the ICCRS website, iccrs.org.

3. Pope St. John Paul II, *Dives in Misericordia*, 13.

4. Chuck Hornsby, "Understanding and Exercising the Gift of Prophecy" (Locust Grove, VA: National Service Committee).

5. See National Service Committee, *Charisms* (Locust Grove, VA: National Service Committee, 2009), nsc-chariscenter.org.

6. Adapted from John and Therese Boucher, *Sharing the Faith That You Love* (Frederick, MD: Word Among Us, 2014), 49.

7. Hillary of Poitiers, Tract on Psalm 64:14, 15, quoted in Kilian McDonnell and George Montague, eds., *Fanning the Flame: What Does Baptism in the Holy Spirit Have to Do with Christian Initiation?* (Collegeville, MN: Liturgical, 1991), 17.

8. Sherry A. Weddell, *Becoming a Parish of Intentional Disciples* (Huntington, IN: Our Sunday Visitor, 2015), 15.

9. Prayer attributed to St. Isidore of Seville (560–636) by Bernard V. Brady. *Essential Catholic Social Thought* (Maryknoll, NY: Orbis, 2008), 112.

10. Patti Gallagher Mansfield, *As by a New Pentecost: The Dramatic Beginning of the Catholic Charismatic Renewal* (Steubenville, Ohio: Franciscan University Press, 1992), 86.

11. Andrew Downie, "Behind Brazil's Catholic Resurgence, *Time*, May 8, 2007, http://content.time.com/time/world/article/0,8599,1618439,00.html.

12. "Prayer of Pope John XXIII to the Holy Spirit for the Success of the Ecumenical Council," in Walter Abbott, SJ, ed., *Documents of Vatican II* (New York: Guild, 1966), 793.

13. Decree on the Apostolate of Lay People, 3, in Austin Flannery, OP, gen. ed., *Vatican Council II: The Conciliar and Post Conciliar Documents* (Northport, NY: Costello, 1998), 769.

14. Pope Paul VI, To Participants in the Third International Congress of the Catholic Charismatic Renewal, May 19, 1975, quoted in Killian McDonnell, OSB, *Open the Windows: The Popes and Charismatic Renewal* (South Bend, IN: Greenlawn, 1989), 11–12. The pope quotes *L'Osservatore Romano*, October 17, 1974.

15. Cited in "How do leaders in the Church view the Catholic Charismatic Renewal?" http://www.rockforddiocese.org/charismaticrenewal/Charismatic%20Renewal/Church%20Views%20and%20Statements.htm.

16. Pope St. John Paul II, Address to the Council of the International Catholic Charismatic Renewal Office, March 14, 1992, 3.

17. Address of His Holiness Benedict XVI to Participants in a Meeting Organized by the Catholic Fraternity of Charismatic Covenant Communities and Fellowships, October 31, 2008.

18. See Austen Ivereigh, *The Great Reformer: Francis and the Making of a Radical Pope* (New York: MacMillan, 2015), 290.

19. Dialogue between Pope Francis and Eugenio Scalfari, "The Pope: How the Church Will Change," *La Repubblica,* October 1, 2013.

20. Keith A. Fournier, "A Current of Grace: Address of Pope Francis to the Charismatic Renewal Conference in Rome," Catholic Online, www.catholic.org.

21. United States Conference of Catholic Bishops, "Grace for the New Springtime: A Statement from the United States Catholic Conference of Bishops on the Charismatic Renewal" (Washington, DC: USCCB, 1997), 1, 2, 4, iccrs.org, quoting "A Pastoral Statement on the Catholic Charismatic Renewal," 1984.

22. "Grace for the New Springtime," 2, quoting Pope St. John Paul II, audience with International Catholic Charismatic Renewal Council, Rome, December 1979.

23. "Grace for the New Springtime," 6.

24. Pope Paul VI, "General Audience," November 29, 1972.

25. Fournier, "A Current of Grace."

26. Pope Francis, Apostolic Exhortation *The Joy of the Gospel*, no. 164, November 24, 2013, vatican.va.

27. ICCRS Doctrinal Commission, *Baptism in the Holy Spirit*, 13, as quoted in National Service Committee, "Fostering Baptism in the Holy Spirit: A Covenant of Understanding," January 9, 2015, nsc-chariscenter.org.

28. Pope Francis addressing the 38th Italian National Convocation of Renewal in the Spirit, July 7, 2014, and quoting Cardinal Leo Josef Suenens, Mass on Pentecost Monday, 1975, Rome, iccrs.org.

29. Pope Francis, 38th Italian National Convocation of Renewal in the Spirit, July 7, 2014.

30. Therese Boucher, A *Prayer Journal for Baptism in the Holy Spirit* (Locust Grove, VA: Chariscenter USA, 2002), 7.

31. Pope Francis, *The Joy of the Gospel*, 120.

32. John Haughey, "The Inconspicuous Third Person: Penetrating the 'Conspiracy of Silence about the Holy Spirit," *New Covenant*, vol. 8, no. 11, May 1979, 5.

33. Homily of Pope Francis, Mass and Canonization of Blessed Fr. Junípero Serra, September 23, 2015.

34. Pope Paul VI, *Evangelii Nuntiandi*, 24.

35. For more about all these steps, see our booklet *Sharing the Faith that You Love* (Frederick, MD: Word Among Us, 2014).

36. George Montague, SM, "Gifts for the Church or Gifts for the Kingdom," *Pentecost Today*, vol. 26, no. 1 (2001), 9–10.

37. Leo Maasburg, *Mother Teresa of Calcutta* (San Francisco: Ignatius, 2011), 194.

38. Anthony F. Chiffolo, *At Prayer with the Saints* (Liguori, MO: Liguori, 1998), 25.

39. Francis MacNutt, "The Essential Baptism of the Holy Spirit," *Pentecost Today*, Winter 2016, 15, nsc-chariscenter.org.

40. Fr. Dave Pivonka, *The Wild Goose*, thewildgooseisloose.com.

41. Pope Benedict XVI, Weekly General Audience, January 13, 2010.

42. Chiffolo, p. 148.

43. Sherry Weddell, *Spiritual Gifts Resource Guide* (Colorado Springs, CO: Siena Institute, 2003), 48, available through siena.org.

44. Pope St. John Paul II, *Christifideles Laici*, 16.

Baptism in the Holy Spirit or Release of the Spirit
A life-transforming breakthrough that enlivens the graces and power of the Holy Spirit received in the sacraments of Christian initiation (baptism, confirmation, and the Eucharist). God grants a new awareness and surrender to the Father, Son, and Spirit and also equips us with charisms for mission and service. (For more see International Catholic Charismatic Renewal Services Doctrinal Commission, *Baptism in the Holy Spirit* [Lost Grove, VA: National Service Committee, 2012], 13.)

Charismatic Prayer Group
A group of people who come together in an informal but regular way for shared prayer, praise, listening to God, faith sharing, and mutual support in Jesus Christ. Participants are united by their experience of being baptized in the Spirit and in the exercise of the charismatic gifts.

Charismatic Prayer Meeting
The informal worship session of a charismatic group. Praise is expressed in a number of ways: songs, formal or spontaneous prayer, silence, even applause and shouts of joy. God may speak to those gathered through Scripture, teaching, exhortation, charismatic gifts like prophecy, and personal sharings.

Charismatic Renewal
(1) A particular movement of God's Spirit that seeks to restore the experience of baptism in the Holy Spirit and the use of charisms in Catholic life, which we designate with capital letters. (2) The experience of ongoing, explicitly charismatic transformation of individuals or groups (no capital letters).

Charisms or Spiritual Gifts
Free gifts of grace given by the Holy Spirit to the faithful. By these gifts, the Spirit makes us able and ready to undertake various tasks for the evangelization, renewal, and upbuilding of the Church and for the salvation of the world.

Conversion

The change in our lives that comes about through the power of the Holy Spirit as we accept the Gospel of Jesus Christ. It is a continuous process in the emotional, intellectual, moral, and social areas of our lives.

Covenant Community

A charismatic group of married and single lay people, religious, and clergy, who formalize their relationships and life together through a solemn agreement grounded in shared, ongoing baptism in the Spirit and daily use of gifts and charisms. Modeled on the early community in the Acts of the Apostles.

Discernment of Spirits

A supernatural instinct by which the Church perceives the origins of seemingly spiritual phenomena, whether human, divine, evil, or a combination thereof; an examination of thoughts, messages, or visions in the light of the Gospel message and Church teaching. Discernment is most fully exercised as an ongoing communal process.

Evangelization

"Bringing the Good News of Jesus into every human situation…. At its essence are the proclamation of salvation in Jesus Christ and the response of a person in faith, which are both works of the Spirit of God" (United States Catholic Bishops, *Go and Make Disciples: A National Plan and Strategy for Catholic Evangelization in the United States,* no. 10, available at usccb.org).

Fruits of the Spirit

Attributes of the Christian life that the Spirit wants to form and perfect in us. The list in Galatians 5:22–23 includes love, joy, peace, patience, kindness, generosity, faithfulness, gentleness, and self-control. For more, read our book *Mending Broken Relationships, Building Strong Ones: Eight Ways to Love as Jesus Loves Us* (Frederick, MD: Word Among Us, 2015).

Gift of Healing

The charism by which people experience physical, emotional, psychological, and spiritual wholeness flowing from God's Spirit and sometimes through hands placed on them in prayer. Healing of memories involves the removal of pain from past hurtful experiences. Healing Masses include a special time of prayer for wholeness along with the use of other charisms.

Laying on of Hands

Placing one's hands on someone's head or shoulder in order to pray for his or her needs.

Life in the Spirit

Living by the guidance and gifts of the Holy Spirit. This term can also refer to the seminar that promotes baptism in the Spirit, using materials like *New Life in the Spirit Seminars Team Manual: Catholic Edition 2000,* which is listed in the Resource Section.

Praying in Tongues

A language of non-rational prayer and song. Praying in tongues is a way of surrendering voice and thoughts to God. Sometimes a message is spoken in tongues to a community and then "interpreted" by another person who has a sense of the meaning of the words or the charism of prophecy.

Prophecy

The speaking forth of a word or communication from God, a kind of private and meaningful message; the charism by which pieces of what God is saying to an individual are offered for the benefit and discernment of the community.

Slain in the Spirit or Resting in the Spirit

An ecstatic experience of God's presence and peace, usually involving a temporary shutdown of abilities like standing and speech.

Witness

A person sharing how God is at work in the details of his or her life, or the telling of personal faith experiences, conversion, healing, and insights for the up building of the community.

The Ark and the Dove, Inc. The mission of this organization is to provide pilgrimages for those baptized in the Holy Spirit and those interested in this grace, retreats for spiritual renewal through the Holy Spirit, and resources for understanding and fostering the charisms. Visit TheArkAndTheDoveWorldwide. org.

Boucher, John and Therese. *Come Holy Spirit*. Video meditation based on St. John of the Cross's prayer "The Living Flame of Love," at youtube.com.

———. *Mending Broken Relationships, Building Strong Ones: Eight Ways to Love as Jesus Loves Us*. Frederick, MD: Word Among Us, 2015. Learn the paths to love, with help from people who have done it.

———. *Sharing the Faith That You Love: Four Simple Ways to Be Part of the New Evangelization*. Frederick, MD: Word Among Us, 2014. Describes the everyday disciple's call to pray, care, share, and dare to invite others to faith in Jesus Christ within the Church.

Boucher, Therese. *New Life in the Spirit Seminars Team Manual: Catholic Edition 2000*. Locust Grove, VA: National Service Committee, 2000. For group learning about charismatic renewal and how to be baptized in the Holy Spirit.

———. *A Prayer Journal for Baptism in the Holy Spirit*. Locust Grove, VA: Chariscenter USA, 2002. Fifty days of meditations and Scriptures uncovering the riches of our heritage in baptism, confirmation, and the Eucharist. Each week focuses on a different name for the Holy Spirit.

Cantalamessa, Fr. Raniero. *Sober Intoxication of the Spirit: Filled with the Fullness of God*, parts one and two. Cincinnati: Servant, 2011, 2012. Discover the power of the Spirit available through the sacraments, by which God purifies and renews us.

Catholic Charismatic Renewal National Service Committee sponsors national conferences and publishes a valuable quarterly magazine called *Pentecost Today,* in addition to leaflets and an online directory of renewal centers and prayer groups across the country. Write Chariscenter USA, P.O. Box 628, Locust Grove, VA 22508-0628, visit nsc-chariscenter.org, or go to "Catholic Charismatic Renewal National Service Committee" on Facebook, or call (800) 338-2445.

Communication Center, a national distributor of Catholic charismatic materials. Visit comcenter.com, call (800) 348-2227, or write Communication Center, 4315 Ralph Jones Court, South Bend, IN 46628.

Congregation for the Doctrine of the Faith. Letter "*Iuvenescit Ecclesia*" to the Bishops of the Catholic Church Regarding the Relationship Between Hierarchical and Charismatic Gifts in the Life and the Mission of the Church, May 16, 2016. http://www.vatican.va/roman_curia/congregations/cfaith/documents/rc_con_cfaith_doc_20160516_iuvenescit-ecclesia_en.html

Ensley, Deacon Eddie. *Sounds of Wonder: 20 Centuries of Prayer in Tongues and Lively Worship in the Catholic Tradition*. Phoenix: Tan, 2013.

Hogan, Fr. Bob, BBD. *Celebrating a Charismatic Jubilee*. Locust Grove, Va.: National Service Committee, Chariscenter USA, 2016. Reflections and insights about what God has done and is doing through the charismatic renewal.

Hornsby, Chuck. "Understanding and Exercising the Gift of

Prophecy." Locust Grove, VA: National Service Committee. Leaflet is available from Chariscenter USA, P.O. Box 628, Locust Grove, VA 22508-0628, (800) 338-2445, nsc-chariscenter.org.

International Catholic Charismatic Renewal Services (ICCRS), officially recognized as part of the Pontifical Council for the Laity in 1993, "for the promotion of Catholic Charismatic Renewal." Visit iccrs.org for international newsletters, videos, and news.

International Catholic Charismatic Renewal Services Doctrinal Commission. *Baptism in the Holy Spirit.* Vatican City: ICCRS, 2012. Reviews the biblical, patristic (the Fathers of the Church), theological, and pastoral understanding about baptism in the Holy Spirit in the Catholic Church. Order at (800) 338-2445 or chariscenter@nsc-chariscenter.org.

Mansfield, Patti Gallagher. *As by a New Pentecost: The Dramatic Beginnings of the Catholic Charismatic Renewal,* Golden Jubilee ed. Phoenix: Amor Deus, 2016. Personal accounts of those who attended the Duquesne weekend and some who experienced baptism in the Spirit shortly after this beginning of the renewal in the United States.

McDonnell, Fr. Killian, and Fr. George T. Montague, eds. *Fanning the Flame: What Does Baptism in the Holy Spirit Have to Do with Christian Initiation?* Collegeville, MN: Liturgical, 1991. Study of the early Church's understanding of baptism in the Holy Spirit.

Montague, Fr. George. *Holy Spirit, Make Your Home in Me.* Frederick, MD: Word Among Us, 2008. Meditations on the gift of the Holy Spirit in Scripture, with personal testimonies to show how the Spirit powerfully transforms lives.

National Conference of Catholic Bishops. *Grace for a New Springtime—A Statement of the Ad Hoc Committee for Catholic Charismatic Renewal.* Washington, DC: USCC, March 1997. Pastoral statement affirming charismatic renewal of individuals and of the Church. Available at nsc-chariscenter. org.

National Service Committee of the Catholic Charismatic Renewal, ed. *Charisms.* Locust Grove, VA: National Service Committee, 2009. A collection of articles on the gifts of the Holy Spirit, with questions for personal and group reflection.

"A New Pentecost: The Catholic Charismatic Renewal Movement," a video description of the beginnings and history of the renewal. www.iccrs.org.

Pivonka, Fr. Dave. *The Wild Goose,* a fourteen-segment video series about the work of the Holy Spirit. thewildgooseisloose. com.

Renewal Ministries offers conferences, radio programming, and missions. RenewalMinistries.net.

Whitehead, Charles. *An Invitation to the Spirit-Filled Life: The Promise, the Power, the Gifts, the Fruit.* Frederick, MD: Word Among Us, 2016. Describes the meaning of living in the Spirit. Includes sharing questions for group or personal study and reflection.

Wilkerson, David, with John and Elizabeth Sherrill. *The Cross and the Switchblade.* New York: Berkley, 1962. The inspiring testimony that has led many people to a deeper awareness of God's love and power to save.

ABOUT THE AUTHORS

John and Therese Boucher are workshop presenters, authors and national leaders in Evangelization and in the Catholic charismatic renewal. Both hold a Master's Degree in Religious Education and have been involved in the Charismatic Renewal since the late 1960s. John is the former Director of Evangelization for the Diocese of Trenton, NJ. Therese is the author of the revised *New Life in the Spirit Seminars Team Manual: Catholic Edition 2000* and *A Prayer Journal for Baptism in the Holy Spirit*. For more than thirty-five years they have offered adult faith formation and training for ministries.

Between them they have written many books, including: *Praying for Our Adult Sons and Daughters: Placing Them in the Heart of God; Sharing the Faith that You Love: Four Simple Ways to be Part of the New Evangelization;* and *Mending Broken Relationships, Building Strong Ones: Eight Ways to Love as Jesus Loves Us.* They can be reached at www.catholicevangelizer.com and at www.johnandthereseboucher.com.